Knitted Teddy Bears
dressed with handknits

Tone Takle
Photos: Sidsel Jørgensen
Translation: Carol Huebscher Rhoades

Designer and author: Tone Takle
Photographs: Sidsel Jørgensen
Layout: Donna design, Tove Balas
Translation: Carol Huebscher Rhoades
Printing: CreateSpace.com

ISBN-10: 145059896X
©2010 Books by Tone Takle
www.tonetakle.no/www.tonetakle.com

In accordance with international copyright law and the Norwegian copyright organization, KOPINOR, no part of this book can be copied or reproduced by any means.

Copying from this book is not permitted in any form or medium in accordance with the regulations pertaining to creative work or agreements about copying determined by KOPINOR, the organization for the rights of cultural property. Copying contrary to these regulations and agreements is an infringement that can lead to prosecution and seizure of materials, and punishment including fines and incarceration.

Table of Contents

Foreword	4
Before You Knit	7
Abbreviations	9
Measurements for the Bears	11
Bear Basics	13
How to Knit the Bears	17
Clothes for Your Bear	25
Undergarments –	
Undershirts	26
Underpants	28
Boxer Shorts	29
Sweaters	31
Overalls	35
Jackets	38
Jogging Pants	41
Shoes and Socks	44
Bear Dress	46
Tunics and Dress	52
Pants	55
Coat	56
Knitting Techniques	63
Acknowledgements	65
Resources	66
Your own Notes	67

Foreword

Giving someone a handknit item is a kind gesture that makes the gift extra special for the person receiving it. It is fun to knit teddy bears and comforting to think that the bear can become a beloved friend for the child who receives it. The bears in this book are made with natural materials that are safe to play with and are an environmentally friendly alternative to the ones you find in toy shops.

I hope everyone using this book will enjoy it. Many of you are experienced knitters while others are beginners. But everyone knows small children who would be happy to have a handmade, soft and nice teddy bear. Writing this book has made me very happy and I recognized the small child in me when I thought about what the bears would look like and which clothes they should have. I hope this book will be easy to use for both new and experienced knitters alike. I have tried as best I can to make the instructions easy to understand. Perhaps I have explained too much for experienced knitters. I hope you will forgive me for that because I want the book to be useful for "new" knitters also.

I have written the patterns so that they can be worked with a wide variety of yarn. Most knitters usually have some "stash" yarn left over from previous projects. Many of the patterns in the book used only about ¾ to 1 ounce / 20-30 g of yarn so check your leftovers and see how you can use them. Good luck! I hope that those who use this book will enjoy knitting the teddy bears and their clothes, and I am sure you will delight everyone around you with the finished bears.

With best wishes,
Tone

Before You Knit

I know a lot of knitters. Very few of them knit gauge swatches before beginning a project. However, knitting gauge is very important. The advantage of a gauge swatch is that it lets you know if you are knitting too tightly or too loosely. Eventually your hands will be experienced enough to sense what is suitable.

The bears in this book will be felted in the washing machine before the body and head are joined. Knitters knit differently and washing machines wash differently and the bears and their clothes are knit from many types of yarn. That makes it difficult to set precise measurements for how big each bear should be and how long the skirt of a dress should be, etc.

The most important aspect is that the width and length of the bears and their clothes are in proportion. For that reason, I've written all the measurements in the instructions in stitches and rows instead of gauge and inches/centimeters. Knit the bear first, working the head and body separately. Felt it in the washer, stuff the pieces with wool, and then sew them together.

Look at the measurement chart for small, medium, and large bears, and pick the size that is closest to the size of the bear you've made. Choose the patterns in that size when you make the clothes.

The patterns for the bear clothes should be considered as starting points for your own style of expression. Make an outfit of dress, sweater, and short or long pants to suit your own taste.

The choice of colors can definitely affect the style of a garment. See, for example, the blue dress on page 30. It is made from the same pattern as the dress in light pastels on pages 50 and 51.

"Yardage" is an important word in this book. Look at the band of paper (ball band) wrapped around the yarn ball when you buy it at the shop. It tells you how many yards/meters are in a ball weighing 1 ¾ or 3 ½ oz / 50 or 100 grams. Let's use Mandarin Petit and Fine Alpaca as examples because many of the clothes in this book are knit with these yarns. Mandarin Petit is 100% cotton with 197 yds / 180 meters in a 50 gram ball. Fine alpaca, a 100% alpaca yarn, has 183 yds / 167 meters in 50 grams. When the pattern states that you need 175-200 yds / 160-180 meters it means that either of these two yarns or something you have on hand within these yardages can be used for the garment.

> **YARDAGE**
> The patterns in this book do not specify a gauge or the particular yarn that the garment should be knit with. Instead, the patterns indicates the size of yarn by listing how much yardage per 50 g ball you'll need so that the garment size will match the one shown in the book.

If you want to use a heavier yarn, for example, one with 115 yds / 105 meters in 50 grams, you have to knit with bigger needles. The garment will be larger than the one shown in the photos but the jacket or pants will still look like a jacket or pants, because the patterns are based on the relation of stitches and rows, not inches/centimeters.

You can also make the bears smaller or larger than those listed in the measurement chart. Use yarn suitable for US 11 / 7 mm needles, for example (and of course knit with US 11 / 7 mm needles) and the bear will be bigger than those shown in the book. Use larger yarn and needles for the bear's garments also.

Some advice about knitting, especially for beginners

Making knit garments that are smooth and even can be difficult for new knitters. It helps to be especially mindful of how tightly you hold the yarn between the fingers of your left hand for continental style or your right hand for American/British style knitting. The yarn should "move" evenly between the fingers. If you hold the yarn too tightly, the stitches will also be too tight. If you hold the yarn too loosely, the stitches will be loose and uneven.

Gauge

Do you knit tightly or loosely? By going up or down in needle size, you can regulate the gauge at which you knit. Personally I knit loosely. If you know that you knit too tightly, go up a needle size from that recommended in the patterns here. Experiment.

Superwash

Wool yarn that has been processed as superwash works well for garments that you plan to wash often in the machine but it won't work for the bears. The wool fibers in the superwash yarn are covered with a substance that looks like resin, and that prevents the wool from shrinking or, in other words, it won't felt very easily. Look at the yarn content information when choosing some for the bear and avoid yarn that is not made of natural materials or has been treated to resist shrinkage.

Fabric Care

When a garment is finished, it is good to block it by steam pressing to smooth out the surface. Place a hand towel over the garment and carefully steam press with low heat. If you don't have a steam iron, dampen the towel first. This type of blocking is good for pure natural materials such as wool and cotton. If you use synthetic yarn, you can adversely affect the handle if you block the garment with steam. It is better, in that case, to lay the garment out under a damp hand towel and let it dry flat. Read the ball band around the yarn. It should indicate whether or not the yarn can be steam pressed.

"Read the whole pattern before you begin knitting" is a statement often found in knitting instructions. In my experience that sometimes makes me even more confused. My recommendation is to work a step at a time so that you'll understand better as you go along. When you have the knitted garment in your hands, and can read the pattern at the same time, it is easier to see what the instructions mean.

If there is a term you don't understand, look it up in the Techniques section. If that doesn't help, you can go the yarn store and ask someone who works there to help you. If it is a good yarn shop, you'll find knitting experts who know a lot about knitting. You can also ask another knitter in the family or your neighborhood. They'll be very happy to help you because they'll think it is wonderful you are knitting. ☺

Abbreviations

beg	begin/beginning
BO	bind off
cm	centimeter(s)
CO	cast on
dpn	double-pointed needles
g	gram(s)
k	knit
k1f&b	knit into front then back of the same stitch to increase
k2tog	knit 2 stitches together to decrease
m	meter(s)
m1	make 1 = lift strand between 2 sts and knit into back loop (an increase)
MC	main color
mm	millimeter(s)
ndl(s)	needle(s)
oz	ounce(s)
p	purl
psso	pass slipped stitch over
rem	remaining
rnd(s)	round(s)
RS	right side – usually the knit surface
Sl	slip
ssk	(slip 1 st knitwise) twice and then knit together into back loops
st(s)	stitch(es)
WS	wrong side – usually the purl surface
yd(s)	yard(s)
yo	yarn over

Note: Yarn ball weights are given in 50 g (1 ¾ ounces) and 100 g (3 ½ ounces).

My good friend Solfrid knitted the brown bear and I knitted the beige one. Solfrid knits beautifully, quite firmly and evenly. I knit more loosely. We used the same size needles and yarn with about the same yardage but ended up with bears that are rather different in size. Solfrid knitted the white dress for her bear in size medium. If I had knit the same dress with the same needles and yarn, it would have been larger. It is an advantage to have the patterns in stitches and rows instead of inches/centimeters. If the same person knits both the bear and the garments, the clothes should fit the bear well no matter whether s/he knits tightly or loosely.

Measurements for the Bears

	SMALL BEAR	**MEDIUM BEAR**	**LARGE BEAR**
Total length	10-10 ¾ in 25-27 cm	11 ½-13 ¾ in 29-35 cm	15 ¾-17 ¼ in 40-44 cm
Circumference around stomach	7-8 in 18-20 cm	10-10 ¾ in 25-27 cm	11 ½-12 ¾ in 29-32 cm
Length of leg (where foot begins)	approx 2 ¾ in approx 7 cm	approx 3 ½ in approx 9 cm	approx 4 ¾ in approx 12 cm
Circumference around leg (open leg width)	5 ¼ in 13 cm	6 in 15 cm	7 in 18 cm
Arm length (where paw begins)	2 ½ in 6 cm	3 ¼ in 8 cm	4 in 10 cm
Circumference around arm (arms outstretched)	4 in 10 cm	4 ¾ in 12 cm	5 ½-6 ¼ in 14-16 cm

Measurements are approximate

Bear Basics

The patterns for these bears are designed with all the measurements given in stitches and rows. For that reason, you can choose from a variety of yarn types without changing the proportions, regardless of the yarn weight and the needles used.

Needles: You'll need a set of 5 double-pointed needles (dpn) and a long circular in the size suitable for the chosen yarn. It's also advantageous to have a couple extra dpn so you can leave the sts of one leg on them while you knit the other leg.

You'll also need a washing machine and carded wool for stuffing and fine embroidery thread or wool yarn to make the snout, mouth, and eyes.

Make sure that the yarn you are using is not superwash because that won't felt in the washer.

This section gives you an overview of the yarn and needles used for the bears in this book. The information is based on the measurements for small, medium, and large bears listed in the chart on page 11.
The gauge depends on how tightly or loosely you knit. The bear's finished measurements are also affected by how much you felt the bear in the washing machine and how tightly you stuff it.

LARGE BROWN BEAR

Yarn: 1 strand Faerytail from Du Store Alpakka 191 yds / 175 m/50 g and 1 strand Finullgarn from Rauma 191 yds / 175 m / 50 g.
Faerytale brown 722 and beige 720
Finullgarn brown 464 and beige 406

Yarn amount: One ball of each of the brown colors and small amounts of beige.
Needles: US size 8 / 5 mm
Bear's Height: approx 16 ½ in / 42 cm
Stuffing: At least 3 ½ oz / 100 g clean wool, depending on how firmly you want to stuff the bear.

Page 13

LARGE GRAY BEAR

Yarn: One strand Faerytail from Du Store Alpakka and 1 strand Tove from SandnesGarn 175 yds / 160 m/50 g.
Snout, ears and paws are knit with light gray Tove 2641 and light beige Faerytale Alpakka 725.
The rest of the body and head are knit with 1 strand natural brown Tove 2652 and 1 strand gray brown Faerytail alpaca 726.
You'll need about 1 oz / 30 g of each of the gray brown colors and less than .35 oz / 10 g of each of the light.
Yarn amount: 191 yds / 175 m/50 g – Faerytail
191 yds / 175 yds/160 m/50 g – Tove
Needles: US size 8 / 5 mm
Bear's Height: approx 15 ¾ in / 40 cm
Stuffing: about 3 ½ oz / 100 g clean wool

LARGE GRAY BEAR WITH PINK SNOUT AND EARS

Yarn: Handspun 2-ply Villsau (Norwegian wild sheep) wool yarn, combined with a fine mohair Rauma yarn called Plumet.
The ears, paws, and snout are made with a little ball of handspun pale pink and white multicolored yarn.
You'll need about 2.6 oz / 75 g of yarn for this bear.
Needles: US size 8 / 5 mm
Bear's Height: approx 15 ¾ in / 40 cm
Stuffing: about 3 ½ oz / 100 g clean wool

MEDIUM BEIGE BEAR

Yarn: 1 strand Finullgarn beige 406 and 1 strand Plumet light beige 246 (both yarns from Rauma). Snout, ears and paws are knit with white leftover yarns in the same weight as Finullgarn. The beige Plumet yarn is knitted together with the white and the beige yarns.

You'll need about 1 oz / 30 g of yarn for the bear. Plumet has good yardage so you'll need just 1 ball. It's a little lighter than the head color and a bit darker than the snout yarn, so it can be used with both colors.

Yarn amount: 273 yds / 250 m/25 g – Plumet
191 yds / 175 m/50 g – Finullgarn
Needles: US size 4 / 3.5 mm
Bear's Height: approx 13 ½ in / 34 cm
Stuffing: about 2 ½ oz / 70 g clean wool

MEDIUM BROWN BEAR

Yarn: For the body, 1 strand Tove dark brown 3082 from SandnesGarn and 1 strand Plumet brown 2450 from Rauma. Ears, paws and snout made with 1 strand Tove brown 2652 and 1 strand Plumet as for body. You'll need about 1 oz / 30 g yarn for this bear.
Yarn amount: 273 yds / 250 m/25 g – Plumet
175 yds / 160 m /50g Tove
Needles: US size 4 / 3.5 mm
Bear's Height: about 11 in / 28 cm
Stuffing: about 2 ¼ oz / 60 g clean wool

SMALL WHITE BEAR

Yarn: natural white 2-ply yarn from Rauma (2-ply Gammelserie GL401).
You need just .92 oz / 26 g for this little bear.
Yarn amount: 175 yds / 160 m/50 g
Needles: US size 1.5 / 2.5 mm
Bear's Height: approx 9 ¾ in / 25 cm
Stuffing: about 1.4 oz / 40 g clean wool

SMALL LIGHT BROWN BEAR

Yarn: Tove from SandnesGarn, natural brown 2652. A loosely spun 2-ply wool yarn.
You'll need 1 oz / 30 g yarn for this bear.
Yarn amount: 175 yds / 160 m/50 g
Needles: US size 2.5 / 3 mm
Bear's Height: approx 11 in / 28 cm
Stuffing: about 1.4 oz / 40 g clean wool

How to Knit the Bears

The bear head and body are knitted separately and then sewn together at the neck after being felted in the washing machine and stuffed with wool. The inside of the ears, underside of the paws and the snout are knitted in garter stitch and the rest of the bear is stockinette.

Some of the bears have one color for the ears, snout, and paws and another color for the rest of the body. Some bears are single color. To simplify the instructions, the yarn for the snout, paws, and ears will be called the "snout color" and the yarn used for the body is the "main color (MC)."

HEAD

Begin with the snout

- With dpn and snout color, CO 4 sts. Work back and forth in garter st (knit every row) until there are 3 ridges on RS (the cast-on yarn tail hangs at the right side). On the next row, k1f&b into the first and last sts, knitting all sts in between = 6 sts total; knit back.
- K1f&b, k1, k1f&b into the 3rd and 4th sts, k1, k1f&b into last st. Knit back.
- K1f&b into 1st st, k3, k1f&b into each of the 2 center sts, k3, k1f&b into last st = 14 sts total. Knit back.
- K1f&b into 1st st, k5, k1f&b into each of the 2 center sts, k5, k1f&b into last st = 18 sts total. Knit back.
- Knit 2 ridges (= 4 rows)
- K1, (k2tog) 3 times, k4, (k2tog) 3 times, k1 = 12 sts rem. Knit 3 rows.
- K2, k2tog, k4, k2tog, k2. Knit back.
- K2, k2tog, k2, k2tog, k2 = 8 sts rem. Knit back.
- K2, (k2tog) 2 times, k2 = 6 sts rem. Knit back.
- K2tog, k2, k2tog = 4 sts rem. BO and cut yarn, weave in tails on WS.
- Now change to MC and work the head in stockinette.

- With RS of snout facing you, begin at the lower right side where the cast-on tail is hanging. With a dpn (ndl 1), pick up and knit 7 sts up to the widest point of the snout. With another dpn (ndl 2), pick up and knit 7 sts along the side + 2 sts where you bound off 4 sts at the top of the snout. With ndl 3, pick up and knit 2+7 sts from the top of the snout and down to the widest point on the left side of the snout. With ndl 4, pick up and knit 7 sts down towards the neck edge. Purl back over the 32 sts on the needles.
- Knit the 7 sts on ndl 1, k5 on ndl 2, and then k2tog 2 times, k2tog 2 times and k5 on ndl 3, k7 on ndl 4 = 28 sts rem. Turn and purl back.
- Now begin short row shaping: K21 across and turn.
- Sl 1 purlwise, p13; turn.
- Sl 1, k11; turn.
- Sl 1, p9; turn.
- Sl 1, k18. Purl back over the 23 sts; turn.
- Sl 1, k1, k1f&b into 1st st on ndl 2, k2, k1f&b into next st, k3. On ndl 3, k3, k1f&b into next st, k2, k1f&b into last st. K2 on ndl 4; turn.
- Sl 1, p19; turn.

Set Aside sts for the Ears

Use two short lengths of contrast color waste yarn to hold the sts for ears while you knit the rest of the head. Knit the 8 first sts on ndl 2 with contrast color yarn and then slide the sts back to left ndl. Knit all the sts with MC as usual. K1 with MC on ndl 3, and then k8 with waste yarn as for ndl 2. Slide the 8 sts back to the left ndl and knit them again with MC. Later you'll remove the waste yarn so that you can knit the ears. Knit the sts on ndl 4 as usual and then purl back over all 32 sts.

Shaping Back of Head

You can move the sts to a circular ndl while you work the back of the head.

- K28 or until 4 sts rem; turn.
- Sl 1 purlwise, p23; turn.
- Sl 1, k19; turn.
- Sl 1, p15; turn.
- Sl 1, k11; turn.
- Sl 1, p7; turn.
- Sl 1 and knit across.
- Purl back over all sts.

Now finish Back of Head
- *K2tog, k2*; rep * to * around. There should be 24 sts. Purl back.
- *K1, k2tog*; rep * to * around = 16 sts rem. BO purlwise on WS. Cut yarn, leaving a tail long enough for seaming back of head later.

Ears
Use the tip of a knitting needle to remove the waste yarn from one of the ears. Divide the sts over 2 dpn, one set for the back of the ear and the other for the front. The front part of the ear should have 8 sts while the back has 10 sts. Pick up the strand between sts for the back so that you have 10 sts.

The front of the ear is knit in garter st with the snout color. Knit 5 ridges over the 8 sts that are on this part. K2tog at the beginning and end of the next row. Knit back. Dec 1 st on each side the same way on the next row. BO 4 rem sts.

The back of the ear is worked with MC in stockinette. Work 5 rows. Dec 1 st (with k2tog) at beg and end of each of the next 3 rows and then BO. Remove the waste yarn holding the sts for the other ear and make the second ear as for the first.

Finishing the Head
Turn head inside out. Weave in all tails and sew the ears together with WS facing. Sew a few extra stitches on each side of the ears to close up the holes. Fold down the bound-off edge at back of head and sew down from WS.

BODY
The legs and body are knitted first and then the arms. Begin at the sole of the foot:
- With snout color, CO 4 sts. Knit 1 ridge (= 2 rows). On the next row, inc 2 sts by working k1f&b into the first and last sts of the row. Knit back over the 6 sts. Knit 3 ridges.
- Dec on the next row as follows: K2tog, k2, k2tog. Knit 3 rows and then BO. Cut yarn and weave in tails on sole.
- With MC, pick up and knit sts around the edge of the sole as follows: 4 sts on each short end, and 7 sts on each long side of the sole = 22 sts. Divide the sts onto 4 dpn: 4 sts on ndl 1, 7 sts on ndl 2, 4 sts on ndl 3, and 7 sts on ndl 4. Join to work in the round and knit 3 rows.

Shaping the Feet
- K4 on ndl 1; k1, k2tog, k4 on ndl 2; k4 on ndl 3; k4, k2tog, k1 on ndl 4. Knit 1 rnd without decreasing.
- K4 on ndl 1; k1, k2tog, k3 on ndl 2; k4 on ndl 3; k3, k2tog, k1 on ndl 4. Knit 1 rnd.
- K4 on ndl 1; k1, k2tog, k2 on ndl 2; k4 on ndl 4; k2, k2tog, k1 on ndl 4 = 16 sts rem.
- Knit 5 rnds.
- Inc 2 sts on each of the 4 ndls by working k1f&b into the first and last st of each ndl. Knit 18 rnds over the 24 sts on dpn.
- BO the last 3 sts on ndl 3 and the first 3 sts on ndl 4 for the first leg and then work around to bound-off sts. Cut yarn.

- Knit the other leg the same way but finish with BO the 3 last sts on ndl 1 and the 3 first sts on ndl 2 so that the bound-off sections of both legs face each other when the bear's feet point outwards.
- Knit the sts from legs 1 and 2 onto the 4 dpn. The center back, where the legs meet, is now the beginning of the round. Knit to that point and place marker (pm). On the first rnd, divide the sts onto dpn with 9 sts on each needle (= 36 sts).

Shaping the Back of the Body
- Knit 7 sts of ndl 1; turn and sl 1, p13; turn.
- Sl 1 and k12; turn.
- Sl 1, p11; turn. Sl 1, k10; turn.
- Sl 1, p9; turn.
- Sl 1, knit all sts on ndls 4 and 1; turn.
- Sl 1 and purl the sts on ndls 1 and 4; turn. Now knit all the sts around.

The sts on ndls 1 and 4 are the back and those on ndls 2 and 3 are the front of the bear. Inc 2 sts at center front and 2 sts at center back on the next rnd; that is, at the places where ndls 1 and 4 meet and where ndls 2 and 3 meet. Knit 1 rnd. Inc 2 sts at center front and 2 sts at center back once more (= 44 sts). Knit 10 rnds.

Now Work Front and Back Separately
Knit sts on ndl 1; turn. P2tog and purl the rem sts on ndls 1 and 4 and, at the same time, move the sts to one dpn; turn. K2tog and knit rest of sts on ndl. Dec 1 st (with k2tog) at beg of every row until 16 sts rem. Work 2 more rows in stockinette or until you have a total of 10 rows counted from where you began to work the front and back separately. Cut yarn and leave back sts on a ndl while you work the front.

Begin front on a WS row and p2tog and then purl all the sts onto 1 ndl. K2tog at beg of next row. Continue to dec 1 st at beg of every row until 16 sts rem for front. Work 2 more rows in stockinette.

Fold the front and back over the legs so that the body is inside out. Sew the opening between the legs from the WS and weave in all tails. Place the ndls with the shoulder sts with RS facing RS. Begin on the side where the yarn is and use a third ndl to work three-needle bind-off. Insert ndl into the first st on both ndls and knit together as if 1 st. Make another st the same way and then bind off the first st by slipping the first st over the 2nd. Knit together and bind off 3 sts at this side. Place the last st onto the ndl closest to you. Turn work. Knit tog and bind off 3 sts on the other side the same way. Place the st which left on the ndl closest to you. There should now be 9 sts on each of the two ndls. Divide these sts onto 4 dpn. Purl. P2tog at each side so that there are 4 sts on each ndl on the first rnd and then purl 2 rows for the neck and BO. Cut yarns and weave in tails on WS. Turn body right side out.

ARMS

Begin at the lower edge of arm opening arm (underarm) and pick up and knit 24 sts with MC. Hold the bear's body so that the stomach turns towards you when you make the first arm and the back faces you for the other arm. Divide the sts so that there are 6 sts on each ndl = 12 sts for the front and 12 sts on the back. The ndl at the underarm is now on ndl 1, followed by ndls 2, 3, and 4. Knit 6 rnds. On the next rnd, k2tog at the beg of ndl 1 and end of ndl 4. Knit 2 rnds. BO 2 sts at underarm on every 3rd rnd 3 more times.

There should now be 16 sts on the ndls. Divide them evenly with 4 sts on each ndl. Knit 3 rnds. The underside of the paw is knitted separately in garter st. Work the top side (ndls 2 and 3) in stockinette with MC. The pieces will be sewn together later.

Underside of Paw

Work back and forth until you have 4 ridges counted on RS. At beg and end of next row, k2tog and then knit back. K2tog at beg and end of next row = 4 sts rem and then BO.

Top side of Paw

Work 5 rows in stockinette. K2tog at beg and end of next row. Knit 1 row without decreasing. Next, k2tog at beg and end of next row; work 1 more row, and then BO. Turn arm and sew the two parts of the paw together. Cut yarns and weave in tails on WS. Make the other arm the same way.

FINISHING THE BEAR

Wash the body and head of the bear in the washing machine on the delicate cycle at 104°F / 40°C with a mild wool wash. If you have some clothes in the machine at the same time, the bear will felt more easily, but don't put in more than half a load or the bear might felt too much. After the bear has been felted, stuff it with clean wool. If you do this while the bear is still wet after the wash it will be easier to shape the details, like the ears, for example.

Stuffing with Wool

Stuff the feet first with washed and carded wool. Stuff the rest of the legs and the arms and then fill the body. Fill the head with wool but do not put wool in the ears – they should be flat. As you are stuffing the bear, check frequently to make sure the bear is taking shape as you want. Do not stuff the bear too full. It needs to be soft and easy to hold.

Joining

Hold the head above the body and sew the parts together with a length from the yarn you knitted with by sewing a stitch in the body, a stitch in the head, and so on, all around the opening. Sew one stitch from under the chin and up to the top of the snout and down again with the yarn you used to sew the head and body together. Pull it together slightly but not so hard that the stitches are visible. This allows the snout to stick out from the face. Baste between the snout and the rest of the head and pull the yarn a bit so that the snout sticks out correctly. If the head flops back and forth, it can be steadied by sewing stitches all the way around from the head down into the body a little outside the first seam (which attached the head to the body).

Baste the line between the legs and body and between the arms and body so that the arms and legs are easier to move.

Ears

Pull the ears sideways so they are shaped correctly, preferably while the bear is still wet after the felting. Make some small basting stitches between the ears and head so that the wool stuffing doesn't wander up into the ears. The ears should be rounded nicely around the head and the back part should stick out a little above the front part of the ear all the way around.

Eyes

Use the stuffing yarn or embroidery thread in the color you want for the eyes. Insert the needle from the side of the head and up to the point where the first eye should be. Let a little of the yarn tail hang outside the head. Sew three long, vertical stitches next to each other where the first eye should be and then 4-5 horizontal stitches crosswise to the first three stitches. Continue sewing the same way, alternating vertical and horizontal stitches, until the eye has the shape of a half ball. Insert the needle up where the other eye should be and make it the same way. Hide the yarn by sticking the needle out to the side of the head, tighten the yarn a bit, and cut yarn so that the end sinks into the head. Tighten the yarn on the other side of the head (where you first inserted the needle) and cut it so it slides into the head.

Mouth and Snout

Insert a sewing needle in from the side of the head as for making the eyes, leaving a yarn tail outside the head. Sew a triangle with dark yarn on the tip of the snout. Sew the mouth with stem or back stitches down from the triangle and then curving out to each side. See the photos for ideas about how to shape the mouth. This is where you can really set the personality of the bear. It is smiling? Or maybe you have a serious bear? The embroidered stitches will look best if they follow the underside of a ridge on the snout. Pull the ends of the yarn and cut them near the head at both sides so that the ends disappear into the head.

Look at the various bears in this book. They have different expressions depending on how high up their eyes are placed in relation to the snout. Some bears are smiling a little because the mouth turns up a little at each side but others are more serious.

Clothes for Your Bear

Undergarments

Underclothes can be a fine foundation for your teddy bear wardrobe. Here you'll find underpants to go under a girl bear's dresses, boxer shorts for the boys, and an undershirt. Depending on the colors you choose, these items can also become a top and shorts for summertime wear. If you knit the legs longer on the boxer shorts, then you have full-length pants.

We used Rowan's Fine Milk Cotton and Mandarin Petit from SandnesGarn for the boxer shorts and undershirt shown here.

UNDERSHIRT

Yarn: approx 165-200 / 150-180 m / 50 g
Needles: Set of 5 dpn US size 1.5 /2.5 mm and crochet hook US size C / 2.5 mm to crochet edgings around neck and armholes.

Instructions: With dpn, CO 48 (56, 64) sts; join, being careful not to twist cast-on row. Knit 1 rnd, dividing sts 12-14-16 onto dpn. Work 3 rnds of k1/p1 ribbing. If you want a striped shirt, begin stripes now. For example, you can knit 2 rnds stripe color, 2 rnds MC.

Work 14 (20, 24) rnds in stockinette but stop when 3 sts rem on the last rnd. BO 6 sts, k18 (22, 26), BO 6, k18 (22, 26) (stitch counts include the stitch left over after the 6 bound-off stitches on front and back).

Now work the front and back separately. Continue the stripe pattern if you have chosen to do that.

Front: Work back and forth in stockinette for 3 (5, 7) rows (if you are working in stripe pattern, it is more practical to knit from the side where the yarn hangs on each row so that you'll have fewer yarns to weave in at finishing. That might mean 2 purl rows or 2 knit rows one after the other).

Shape neck: K7 (9, 11), BO 4, complete row. Each side of the neck is now worked separately. Work back to the bound-off center sts (neck edge).

Round neck: On the next row, k2tog at neck edge. Dec 1 st at neck edge on every RS row a total of 2 (4, 6) times or until 5 sts rem for shoulder. Work 8 (5, 7) more rows and then BO. Work other side of neck the same way, reversing shaping.

Back: Work 8 (10, 12) rows in stockinette. BO. Sew the straps from the front at each side of the back. Crochet an edging with single crochet around the armholes and neck.

UNDERPANTS TO GO UNDER A DRESS

These "leggings" are a little old-fashioned in style and are lovely under a dress. Make the dress one color and the leggings another so they are noticeable when they stick out from under the edge of the skirt.

For these pastel color underpants, we used Mandarin Petit and Mini Duett from SandnesGarn and Rowan's Purelife Organic Cotton (see also picture page 10).

Yarn: Use yarn recommended for needles US 1.5-2.5 / 2.5 and 3 mm with 165-200 yds / 150-180 m/50 g. You'll also need a short length of elastic band for the waist band.

Needles: Set of 5 dpn US size 1.5/2.5 mm. We recommend 2 extra dpn for holding stitches on the pant legs.

Instructions: CO 48 (56, 64) sts; join and knit 1 round while you divide the sts over four dpn. Purl 1 rnd and then knit 1 rnd.

Make a lace row that can be a casing for elastic band: *Yo, k2tog*; rep * to * around. Knit 1 rnd. The beginning of the rnd is at center back.

Make the pants a little higher at the center back with short rows: K4; turn, p8; turn; k12; turn p16; turn. On the largest size, continue with k20; turn, p24; turn. Knit back to the beginning of the rnd for all sizes. Now knit 2 (3, 4) rnds.

Next rnd: Inc with m1 after the first st, 1 st before and after the 2 center front sts, and before the last st of the rnd. Knit 1 rnd. Inc the same way on every other rnd a total of 4 (5, 7) times. Inc on the next rnd 1 st after the first 2 sts, before and after the 4 sts at center front, and before the last 2 sts of the rnd. Knit 2 rnds. Now knit until 2 sts rem. BO 4 sts, knit until you come to the 4 sts at center front, and BO them. Finish rnd.

Now work each leg separately: 30 (36, 40) sts for each leg. Divide the sts for 1 leg onto 4 dpn. Knit 4 (5, 7) rnds. At beg of each dpn, k2tog (= 4 sts dec). Purl 1 rnd, knit 1 rnd and then BO. Make the other leg the same way. Seam the gap between the legs, weave in all yarn tails on WS and thread elastic band through lace row casing.

BOXER SHORTS AND STRAIGHT LEG PANTS

This pattern can be used for making underpants, shorts and long pants with narrow legs. The pants are worked from the waist down.

Yarn: Use yarn 165-200 yds / 150-180 m/50 g and usually knitted on US size 1.5 and 2.5 /2.5 and 3 mm. You'll also need a short length of elastic band to thread through the lace row at the waist.

Needles: Set of 5 dpn US size 1.5 / 2.5 mm. We recommend 2 extra dpn for holding stitches on the pant legs.

The pants can be knit in a single color or in a stripe pattern; for example, 2 rnds stripe color, 2 rnds MC. Repeat these 4 rnds all the way down.

Instructions: CO 56 (64, 72) sts, join and divide the sts evenly over 4 dpn while you also knit the first rnd. Work garter st in the round: (knit 1 rnd, purl 1 rnd) 3 times.

Now make a lace rnd: *Yo, k2tog*; rep * to * around. Knit 1 rnd. Begin the rnd at center back.

Page 29

Now make the pants a little higher at the center back with short rows: K4; turn, p8; turn; k12; turn p16; turn. On the largest size, continue with k20; turn, p24; turn. Knit back to the beginning of the rnd for all sizes.

If you want striped pants, begin stripes now. Knit 2 (2, 4) rnds. On the next rnd, k1, m1, knit until 1 st rem on ndl 2, m1, k2, m1 on ndl 3 and then knit sts of ndl 4 and m1 before last st, end k1. Knit 3 rnds without increasing. Inc the same way on every 4th rnd 1 (2, 2) more times.

Increase on the next rnd: K2 on ndl 1; m1, knit until 2 sts rem on ndl 2, m1, k2; and m1 after the first 2 sts on ndl 3 and before the last 2 sts on ndl 4. Knit 3 rnds. Knit until 2 sts rem on next rnd. BO 4, knit until 2 sts before center front, BO 4 and knit rem sts.

Now work each leg separately. Divide the sts for one leg evenly over 4 dpn as you knit the first rnd. You can leave the sts for the other leg on a couple of extra dpn.

Boxer Shorts: Knit 4 (4, 6) rnds and then 3 rnds of k1/p1 ribbing. BO in ribbing. Work the other leg the same way.

Long Pants: Knit 14 (22, 34) rnds on each leg. If you want striped pants, knit an extra rnd with MC before working ribbing. Finish with 5 rnds of k1/p1 ribbing. BO in ribbing. Work the other leg the same way. Cut yarn and weave in all tails on WS. Sew the gap between the legs with WS facing. Thread elastic band through lace row casing on pants.

Straight leg pants knitted with Fine Alpaca from Du Store Alpakka. See other examples of straight leg pants on pages 32 and 33.

Sweaters

A

SUGGESTIONS FOR STRIPE PATTERNS

All the sweaters in this book are knit with Fine Alpaca from Du Store Alpakka, Mandarin Petit and Duett Mini from Sandnes-Garn.

A. Blue sweater with white stripes on the previous page is knit with Mandarin Petit from SandnesGarn. Stripe repeat: *3 rnds blue, 1 rnd white.*

B. Blue-green sweater is knit with signal green stripes in Fine Alpaca. Stripe repeat: *4 rnds blue-green, 1 rnd signal green.*

C. Single color sweater with long sleeves in the smallest size. Knit in signal green Fine Alpaca.

D. Red short-sleeved sweater with pink stripes of Fine Alpaca. Stripe repeat: *2 rnds pink, 2 rnds red.*

E. Pink sweater with white stripes on the next page is knit with Sandnes' Duett Mini, SandnesGarn. Stripe repeat: *4 rnds pink, 2 rnds white.*

SHORT- OR LONG-SLEEVED SWEATER

This pattern can be used for both long and short sleeve sweaters or for a vest. Make a stripe pattern or use a single color as you like.

Yarn: Use yarn 165-200 yds / 150-180 m/50 g
Needles: Set of 5 dpn US sizes 1.5 and 2.5 / 2.5 and 3 mm

Instructions: The ribbing is worked with the MC and then you can change to your choice of stripes or single color.

With smaller dpn, CO 48 (56, 64) sts and join to knit in the round as you divide the sts over 4 dpn: 12 (14, 16) sts on each dpn. Work 5 rnds of k1/p1 ribbing.

Change to larger dpn and knit 12 (17, 22) rnds in stockinette, ending when 2 sts rem on final rnd. BO 4, k20 (24, 28), BO 4, k20 (24, 28). When counting sts between the bind-offs, include the st left over from the bind-off on both front and back. Now work the front and back separately. If you've chosen a stripe pattern continue in it.

Front: Work back and forth in stockinette for 3 (5, 7) rows. If you are working a stripe pattern, it is most practical to knit from the side where the yarn is hanging so that you have fewer ends to weave in later. That means sometimes you'll work two purl or two knit rows one after the other.

Shape neck: K8 (10, 12), BO 4, knit rem sts on row. Now work each side of neck separately. Purl back to neck edge at the bound-off center sts.

Page 33

Round the neck: On the next row, k2tog at neck edge. Dec 1 st at neck edge on every RS row a total of 2 (4, 6) times or until 6 sts rem for shoulder. Work 4 (2, 0) more rows and then BO.

Shape neck on other side: K2tog at neck edge on every other row until 6 sts rem for shoulder. Work 4 (2, 0) more rows and then BO.

Back: Work 5 (7, 9) rows in stockinette. BO to shape neck: K8 (10, 11) sts, BO 4 (4, 6), knit rem sts across. Now work each side of neck separately as for front. BO for neck shaping on every RS row 2 (4, 5) times. Work 2 (0, 0) more rows and then BO.

Neckband on both sweaters: With smaller dpn and color 1, pick up and knit 40 (48, 52) sts around neck and begin with 1 rnd of twisted knit (=knit each st into back loop). Now work 2 rnds k1, p1 ribbing and BO in ribbing on next rnd.

VEST: With smaller dpn, pick up and knit 28 (32) 40 sts around one armhole and begin with 1 rnd twisted knit. At the same time, k2tog at beg and end of rnd for largest size. Work 2 rnds k1/p1 ribbing and then BO in ribbing on next rnd. Work the other armhole band the same way. Cut yarn and weave in all tails on WS.

Short and Long Sleeves: With larger dpn, pick up and knit 28 (32) 40 sts around an armhole and begin with 1 rnd twisted knit. For short sleeves, work 5 (10, 15) rnds in stockinette and, for long sleeves, knit 10 (16, 22) rnds.

Long Sleeves: Change to smaller dpn and k2tog at beg of each ndl on the next rnd (= 4 sts dec).

Finishing both Long and Short Sleeves: Change to smaller dpn and work 5 rnds k1/p1 ribbing. BO in ribbing. Make the other sleeve the same way. Weave in all tails on WS.

SCARF

This scarf is easy to knit and can be varied endlessly. Here are the instructions for the scarf shown in the photo.

Yarn: Use yarn 175-200 yds / 160-180 m/50 g. We used Fine Alpaca in green and blue.
Needles: Two dpn or a circular US size 1.5 / 2.5 mm

Green and blue striped scarf: With MC, CO 10 sts and knit 6 ridges (= 12 rows).

Stripe Pattern: 1 ridge CC, 2 ridges MC. We repeated the stripe pattern 30 times. Finish with 4 ridges MC and then BO.

Basic scarf: CO 10 sts and knit 100 ridges and then BO.

Overalls

Yarn: Use yarn 175-200 yds / 160-180 m/50 g.
Needles: Set of 5 dpn and a short circular US sizes 1.5 and 2.5 / 2.5 and 3 mm. If you want to crochet an edging around the neck and armholes, you'll also need a crochet hook US size C / 2.5 mm.

Instructions: Begin at lower edge of one leg. With smaller dpn, CO 28 (32, 40) sts; join, being careful not to twist cast-on row and knit 7 rnds. Change to larger dpn. On the first rnd, inc with k1f&b into every 4th st = 35 (40, 50) sts. Knit 3 rnds. On the next rnd, inc with k1f&b into every 5th st = 42 (48, 60) sts. Knit 16 (20, 24) rnds. BO 4 (6, 8) sts at beg of next rnd and, at the same time, knit rem sts onto short circular. Make the other leg the same way.

Now place the sts of both legs onto short circular, with the bound-off sections facing each other; knit all the leg sts on the next rnd. Knit 2 more rnds = 76 (84, 104) sts total.

Dec 2 sts at center front and 2 sts at center back on every other rnd 3 (3, 4) times. After these dec rnds, 64 (72, 88) sts rem. Knit 3 (7, 15) rnds.

Change to smaller circular and dec: *k2, k2tog*; rep * to * around = 48 (54, 66) sts rem. Knit 5 (7, 7) rnds.

On the next rnd, dec as follows: K9 (9, 11), BO 31 (36, 44) and k9 (9, 11) and then knit around until you reach bound-off sts. Purl back over all the sts = 17 (18, 22) sts rem.
K2tog at beg and end of next row = 15 (16, 20) sts rem. Work 1 (3, 3) rows in stockinette.

Shape Straps: K5, BO 5 (6, 10), k5. Now work each strap separately in stockinette. Tighten the first and last st on each row a bit so the strap edges will be neat. Work 18 (24, 30) rows on each strap or until it is the right length (try overalls on the bear as you work). BO.

Sew the straps down at the edge of the back. Weave in all tails on WS and seam the gap between the pant legs.

Crochet Edgings: If you like, using the yarn you knit with or another color, work a round of single crochet around the neck and armholes. This prevents the straps from rolling in to the WS.

The overalls in the book are knit with Mandarin Petit and Sandnes Mini Duett, both yarns from SandnesGarn.

Page 37

Jacket

You can knit this jacket in soft colors for a feminine look or make it sturdy enough for a sailor with navy blue and brass buttons. There's a huge assortment of colors and yarn you can use. You can also choose a round or straight collar.

Yarn: We've used a thicker yarn for the jacket than for the other garments in the book. The instructions work for both wool and cotton yarns with about 115-131 yds / 105-120 m/ 50 g (usually knit on ndls US sizes 2-4 / 3 and 3.5 mm). You'll need 2 balls of yarn for the largest size jacket.

Needles: Circular US sizes 2.5 and 4 / 3 and 3.5 mm + crochet hook US size C / 2.5 mm if you want a single crochet edging.

Notions: 2-4 buttons.

Before you begin: The jacket is knit cuff to cuff in two pieces. Each piece consists of a sleeve, half the back and one side of the front. The two pieces are sewn together down the back and under the sleeves; the collar is knit on afterwards.

Instructions: With smaller ndls, CO 20 (22, 24) sts and knit 2 ridges (= 4 rows). Inc on the next row as follows: *K1, k1f&b in next st*; rep * to * across = 30 (33, 36) sts. Knit back over all the sts.

Change to larger ndls and knit 9 (12, 18) ridges. At beg of the next 2 rows, CO (Knitted CO) 6 (8, 12) sts and knit the rem sts of row as usual for both rows = 42 (49, 60) sts. Knit 3 (3, 5) ridges as counted on RS.

Shape Neck: K19 (23, 28), BO 4 (3, 4) and k19 (23, 28). Now finish the back. Work back to the bound-off sts; turn. K2tog and knit rem sts across. Rep this row once more for the two largest sizes. Knit 5 (5, 6) ridges over the 18 (21, 26) sts rem for back and then BO as you work the last row.

Front: Begin at neck edge. K2tog at beg of every neck edge row on the next 4 (5, 7) ridges = 15 (18, 21) sts rem.

On the first front piece, make the buttonholes. Begin at the top at the neckline. Work *k2, yo, ssk*; rep * to * once more or several times if you want more than two

The dark blue jacket with brass buttons is knit with Rauma's 3-ply 100% wool yarn. A 50 g ball has 115 yds / 105 m.

Page 39

buttons for the jacket. Knit the rem sts of row. Knit back over all the sts and then BO.

Knit the other half of the jacket the same way, knitting a complete row over all the sts instead of working buttonholes. BO. Weave in all yarn tails on WS and sew the jacket down the back, under the sleeves and at the sides.

Round Neck without Collar: With crochet hook US C / 2.5 mm, work a row of single crochet along the front and neck edges.

Round Collar: With smaller dpn and the same yarn as for jacket, pick up and knit sts with WS facing: Pick up sts along the diagonal sides of the front on one side of the front, along the back neck and then down the diagonal section of the other front. Pick up 24 (26, 28) sts on each half of the jacket for a total of 48 (52, 56) sts.

Knit 2 rows. Knit next row until 2 sts rem; turn. Knit until 2 sts rem on the other side of the collar; turn. The places where you've turned make a little gap between the stitches. Knit each row until 2 sts before the gap of the collar until you can count 3 (4, 4) gaps on each side. Now knit back over all the sts to the point where you began picking up sts for the collar. BO the first 3 sts at beg of the next two rows. BO the first 2 sts at beg of the next 6 (6, 8) rows. BO rem sts, binding off loosely enough so collar is flexible. Weave in all yarn tails on WS.

With crochet hook US C / 2.5 mm, make a row of single crochet along the collar edge. Use the yarn you knit with or a contrasting color.

Straight Collar: With smaller ndls and jacket yarn, pick up and knit sts as for round collar = 48 (52, 56) sts total.

Knit 2 ridges. BO the first 4 sts on the next two rows. Knit 4 ridges.

Change to larger ndls and knit 1 ridge. BO loosely. Sew on buttons.

The yellow jacket is knit with Rowan Purelife Organic Cotton (131 yds / 120 m/50 g).

The pink jacket is knit with Sublime, a blend of Merino wool, silk and cashmere (127 yds / 116 m/50 g).

Jogging Pants

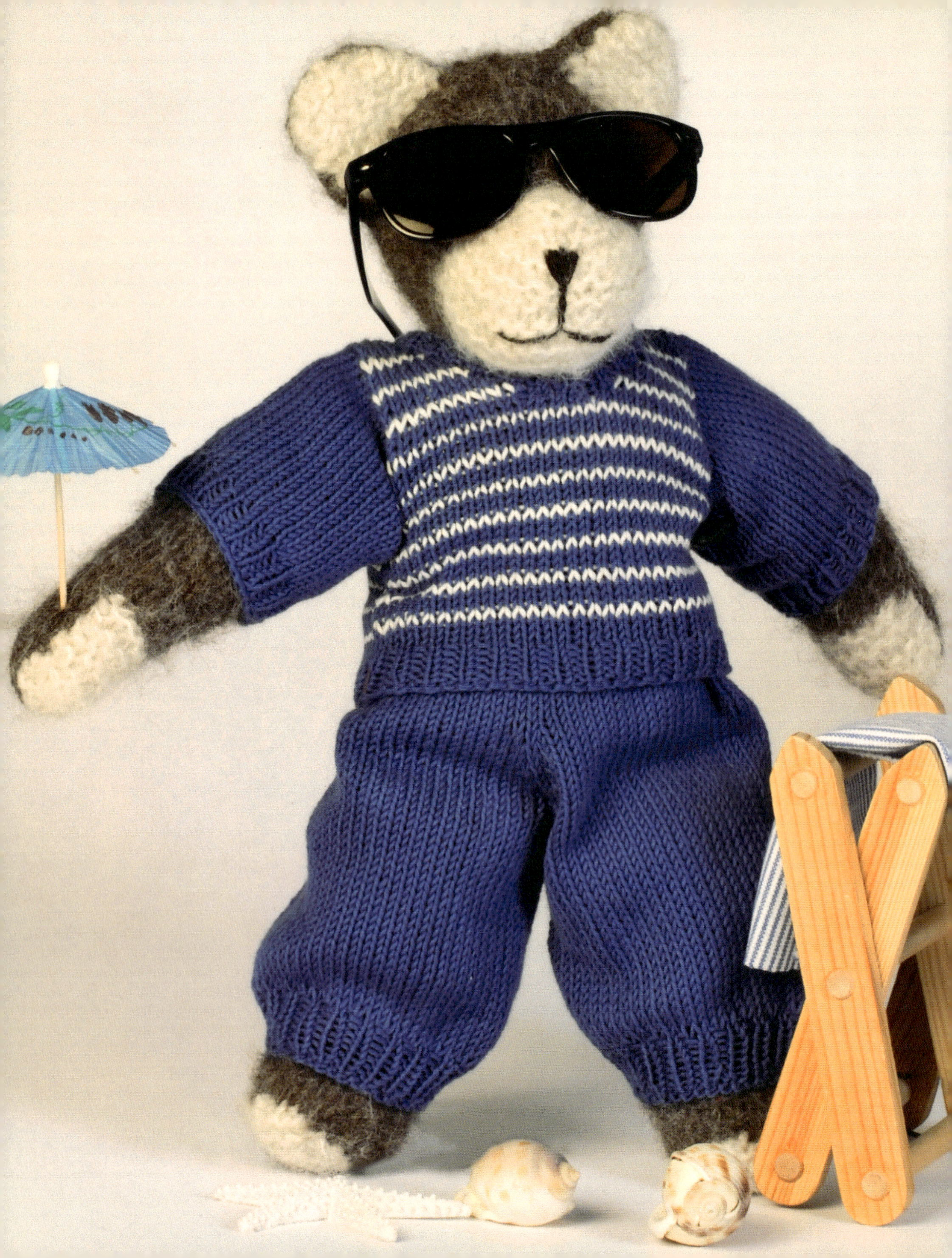

The striped sweater and pants are knit with the same yarn to make a set – perhaps a jogging outfit? Make the top following the basic sweater pattern with short or long sleeves and combine it with the pants described below.

Yarn: 175-200 yds / 160-180 m/50 g

Needles: Set of 5 dpn US sizes 1.5 and 2.5 / 2.5 and 3 mm and a short circular in those sizes for the two largest size outfits. It is also useful to have 2 extra US 2.5 / 3 mm dpn if you don't have the short circular so that you can hold sts of one leg while you work the other leg.

Notions: elastic band long enough to go around bear's waist.

Instructions: With smaller dpn, CO 28 (32, 40) sts; join and knit 1 rnd as you divide the sts onto dpn. Work 7 rnds k1/p1 ribbing.

Change to larger dpn and, on the first rnd, inc 1 st with k1f&b in every other st = 42 (48, 60) sts total. Knit 20 (24, 28) rnds. BO 4 (6, 8) sts at beg of next rnd and then knit rem sts as usual.

For the two larger sizes, you can move the sts to the short circular.
Make another leg the same way.

Place the two legs with the bound-off sections facing each other and join on the next rnd. Knit 2 more rounds = 76 (84, 104) sts total.

K2tog twice at center front and center back on every other rnd 3 (3, 4) times = 64 (72, 88) sts rem. Knit 3 (5, 7) rnds.

Change to smaller ndl and *k2, k2tog*; rep * to * around = 48 (54, 66) sts rem. Knit 3 rnds.

Make a lace rnd for the elastic casing. K0 (2, 2), *yo, k2tog*; rep * to * around. Knit 1 rnd, purl 1 rnd and then BO.

Weave in tails on WS and seam the gap where the legs meet.

Thread elastic band through pants' lace row casing.

The jogging pants and sweater are knit with the same yarn. The sweater stripe repeat is: 3 rounds MC (blue), 1 rnd CC (natural white). The ribbed edges are knit with the main color (blue) as are the pants. We used SandnesGarn's Mandarin Petit.

Shoes and Socks

These shoes and socks are knitted in one piece so it's easy for the little ones to take them off and on.

Yarn: Use yarn recommended for needles US 1.5 and 2.5 / 2.5 and 3 mm with 175-200 yds / 160-180 m/50 g. Two colors, one for the socks and one for the shoes. You might want a third color for the soles under the shoes.
Needles: Set of 5 dpn US size 1.5 / 2.5 mm

Instructions With sock color, CO 32 (36, 40) sts; join and knit 1 rnd while you divide the sts onto the four dpn. Knit 3 rnds in k1/p1 ribbing.

Knit 1 rnd in stockinette, k2tog at beg and end of the first rnd. Knit 2 rnds without dec; rep * to * 1 (2, 3) more times = 28 (30, 32) sts rem. Cut yarn.

Change to shoe color and knit 1 rnd and then purl 1 rnd as you divide the sts 9 (10, 10) sts on ndl 1, 10 (10, 12) sts on ndl 2, and 9 (10, 10) sts on ndl 3. Set ndl 4 aside for now.

Now work back and forth only on sts of ndl 2: Work two rows without dec in sock color. K2tog at beg and end of the next row and then purl 1 row without decreasing.

Change to shoe color and k2tog at beg and end of the next row. Knit back (= 1 ridge with gray) and then k2tog at beg and end of the next row; knit back and then BO.

Cut yarn and begin the next row at the center back with shoe color as it will be visible where row usually begins. First knit 1 row. Knit the 9 (10, 10) sts of ndl 1, pick up and knit 6 (6, 8) + 6 (6, 8) sts with the 2 empty dpn and then knit the sts on the last dpn; join to work in the round. Purl the next rnd so that it makes 1 ridge and then continue alternating knit and purl rnds for 4 (6, 8) more rnds or until you can count 4 (5, 6) ridges on the back of the shoe.

The rest of the rnds are worked in stockinette and you can change color here if you want another color on the sole. **First round: *K2tog, k2*; rep * to * around. Knit 2 rnds without decreasing**. Rep ** to ** once more and then BO on the last rnd.

These decreases don't go all the way up on all the sizes but it is important that the sole is even all around. With WS facing, seam bottom of foot and weave in all yarn tails on WS.

For these shoes and socks, we've used Mini Duett from SandnesGarn. These take so little yarn that you can easily find leftover yarns to knit them.

Page 45

Bear Dress

This dress takes on a modern or nostalgic style depending on what colors and materials you choose to knit with. Your bear will look perky in a deep blue dress, straight leg pants, and a pink and red sweater. For a romantic and sweet outfit, knit with a light color cotton.

Yarn: 175-200 yds / 160-180 m/50 g
Needles: I used dpn US size 1.5 / 2.5 mm and a short circular. If you usually knit tightly go up a needle size to US 2.5 / 3 mm. It is important to knit this type of pattern firmly so the pattern looks its best. You'll also need a crochet hook US size C / 2.5 mm for single crochet edgings around the neck and armholes.

Patterns A, B, and C are described on page 48-49.

Instructions: CO 112 (128, 144) sts; join, being careful not to twist cast-on row. Knit 1 rnd, purl 1 rnd.

Skirt, small size: Work pattern C once. On the next rnd, *k1, k2tog, k3, ssk*; rep * to * around = 48 sts rem for small size.

Skirt, medium: First work pattern B and then rnds 1-18 of pattern C.
Next rnd: *K1, k2tog, k5*; rep * to * around = 56 sts for medium size.

Skirt, large: Work pattern A then B and finish with rnds 1-18 of pattern C = 64 sts for large size.

All three sizes:
There should be 48 (56, 64) sts. Knit around in stockinette for 5 (7, 9) rnds.
Knit around until 2 sts rem and then BO 4 sts, k20 (24, 28), BO 4 and knit rem sts of rnd.

Work back and front separately.

Front: Work back and forth in stockinette for 3 (5, 7) rows.

Shape Neck: K8 (10, 12), BO 4, knit rem sts on rnd. Now work each side of the neck separately. Work back to neck edge at bound-off center sts.

Low Rounded Neck: On the next row, sl 1-k1-psso, Dec 1 st the same way on every RS row at neck edge a total of 2 (4, 6) times or until 6 sts rem for shoulder. Work 4 (2, 1) more rows and then BO.

Neck shaping on other side: Begin at neck edge and purl across. On the next row, (RS), knit the last 2 sts tog. Dec the same way on every RS row at neck edge until 6 sts rem for shoulder. Work 4 (2, 1) more rows and then BO.

Back: Begin at WS and work in stockinette for 5 (7, 9) rows.

Shape back neck: K8 (10, 11), BO 4 (4, 6) and then knit rem sts of row. Now work each side of back neck separately as for front. Dec at neck edge on every other row 2 (4, 5) times and then work 2 (2, 1) rows more and BO.

Weave in all tails on WS and join the shoulders. Make a row of single crochet around the neck and armhole edges.
Finish by steam pressing the dress under a damp towel. This will improve the look of the skirt pattern.

Page 47

Pattern A (repeat * to * around)
Rnd 1: *P11, k3, yo, ssk, k2.*
Rnd 2: Knit.
Rnd 3: *P11, k1, k2tog, yo, k1, yo, ssk, k1.*
Rnd 4: Knit.
Rnd 5: *P11, k2tog, yo, k3, yo, ssk.*
Rnd 6: *K2tog, k7, ssk, k7.*

Pattern B (repeat * to * around)
Rnd 1: *P9, k3, yo, ssk, k2.*
Rnd 2: Knit.
Rnd 3: *P9, k1, k2tog, yo, k1, yo, ssk, k1.*
Rnd 4: Knit.
Rnd 5: *P9, k2tog, yo, k3, yo, ssk.*
Rnd 6: *K2tog, k5, ssk, k7.*

Pattern C (repeat * to * around)
Rnd 1: *P7, k3, yo, ssk, k2.*
Rnd 2: Knit.
Rnd 3: *P7, k1, k2tog, yo, k1, yo, ssk, k1.*
Rnd 4: Knit.
Rnd 5: *P7, k2tog, yo, k3, yo, ssk.*
Rnd 6: *K2tog, k3, ssk, k7.*

There should now be 96 sts around.

Rnd 7: *P5, k3, yo, ssk, k2.*
Rnd 8: Knit.
Rnd 9: *P5, k1, k2tog, yo, k1, yo, ssk, k1.*
Rnd 10: Knit.
Rnd 11: *P5, k2tog, yo, k3, yo, ssk.*
Rnd 12: *K2tog, k1, ssk, k7.*

There should now be 80 sts around.

Rnd 13: *P3, k3, yo, ssk, k2.*
Rnd 14: Knit.
Rnd 15: *P3, k1, k2tog, yo, k1, yo, ssk, k1.*
Rnd 16: Knit.
Rnd 17: *P3, k2tog, yo, k3, yo, ssk.*
Rnd 18: *Sl 1-k2tog-psso, k7.*

There should now be 64 sts around.

Rnd 19: *P1, k3, yo, ssk, k2.*
Rnd 20: Knit.
Rnd 21: *P1, k1, k2tog, yo, k1, yo, ssk, k1.*
Rnd 22: Knit.
Rnd 23: *P1, k2tog, yo, k3, yo, ssk.*
Rnd 24: Knit.

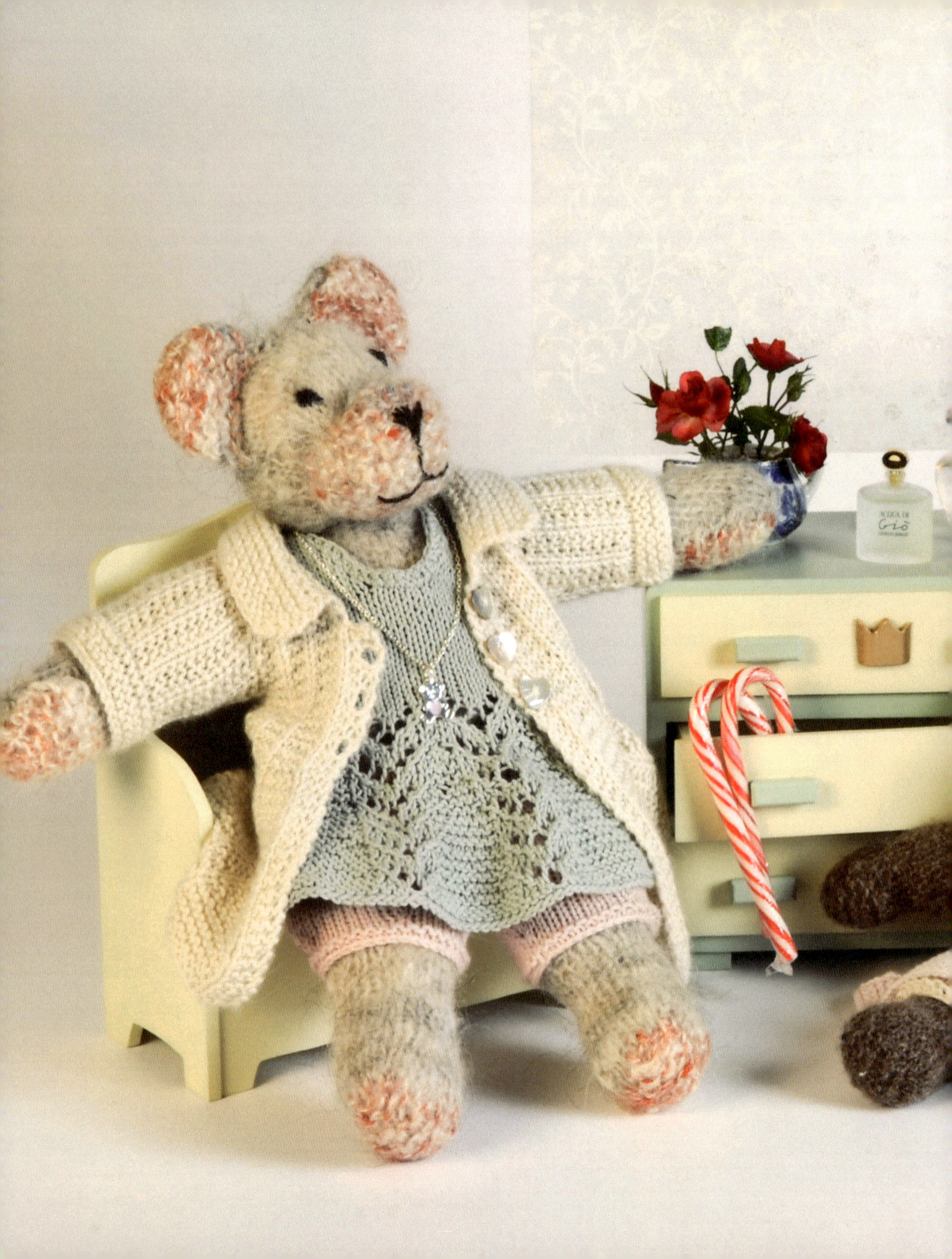
Giò

These sweet pastel dresses are knit with Rowan's 4-ply cotton yarn with 186 yds / 170 m/50 g.

Tunic

TUNIC AND PANTS FOR A GIRL BEAR – AND A DRESS

With soft yarn colors and a flower pin, this outfit with Capri length pants and a lace tunic is so very feminine. By lengthening the tunic, you can adapt this pattern to make a sweet dress – or, perhaps, a nightdress?

Yarn: Yarn recommended for needles US sizes 1.5 and 2.5 / 2.5 and 3 mm; 175-200 yds / 160-180 m/50 g
Needles: Short circular and set of 5 dpn in US sizes 1.5 and 2.5 / 2.5 and 3 mm
Notions: Short length of elastic for waistband and flower pin

Before you begin: The tunic is knit beginning at lower edge and the sleeves are added last. The legs are knit separately for the pants and then the rest is knit in one piece. The dress is made following the same instructions as for the tunic but has been lengthened.

Pattern for Tunic/Dress
Rnd 1: K3, *yo, sl 1-k1-psso, k6. * Rep * to *, ending last rep with k3 instead of k6.
Rnd 2: Knit.
Rnd 3: K1, *k2tog, yo, k1, yo, sl 1-k1-psso, k3.* Rep * to *, ending last rep with k2 instead of k3.
Rnds 4-6: Knit.

Tunic/Dress
Instructions: With larger size circular, CO 128 (144, 160) sts; join, being careful not to twist cast-on row. Knit 3 rnds. On the next rnd, k2 tog around = 64 (72, 80) sts rem. Knit 4 rnds.

Work in pattern as described above 2 (3, 4) times for the tunic and 4 (5, 7) times for the dress. On the next rnd, dec to 48 (56, 64) sts as follows: *K 2 (alternately 2 and 3 sts, 3), k2tog.* Rep * to * around.
Change to smaller circular and knit 2 (3, 4) rnds. On next rnd, knit until 2 sts rem and then BO 4 sts, k20 (24, 28), BO 4 and knit rest of rnd.

Now work the back and front separately.
Front: Work back and forth in stockinette for 3 (5, 7) rows.

Shape neck: K8 (10, 12), BO 4, knit rest of row. Now work each side of neck separately. Purl back to neck edge at center bound-off sts.

Neck Shaping: On the next row, sl 1-k1-psso. Dec the same way at neck edge on every RS row a total of 2 (4, 6) times or until 6 sts rem for shoulder. Work another 4 (2, 0) rows in stockinette and then BO.

Neck Shaping on Opposite Side: Begin at neck edge and purl across WS. On the next row, knit until 2 sts rem and k2tog. Dec at neck edge on every RS row until 6 sts rem. Work another 4 (2, 0) rows in stockinette and then BO.

Back: Beginning on WS, work 5 (7, 9) rows in stockinette.

Shape Back Neck: on RS, K8 (10, 11), BO 4 (4, 6) and knit rem sts across. Now work each side of neck separately as for front. Dec at neck edge on every RS row 2 (4, 5) times. Work another 2 (0, 0) rows in stockinette and then BO.
Weave in all yarn tails on WS and then join shoulders.

Page 53

Neckband: With smaller dpn, pick up and knit 40 (48, 52) sts around neck. Knit 1 rnd, purl 1 rnd, and then work 1 rnd in k1/p1 ribbing. Knit 1 rnd as follows: (K6, k2tog) around (this rep doesn't work evenly for the largest size: end rnd with k4). BO. This edging turns the band in so it won't flare out.

For a sleeveless tunic/dress: With smaller dpn, pick up and knit 28 (32, 40) sts around armhole; join. Knit 1 rnd, purl 1 rnd and BO knitwise.

Sleeves: With larger dpn, pick up and knit 28 (32, 40) sts around armhole; join. Knit 10 (16, 22) rnds. Change to smaller dpn and k2tog at beg of every needle (= 4 sts dec). Knit 1 rnd, purl 1 rnd and then work 1 rnd of k1/p1 ribbing. End with 3 knit rnds and then BO.

PANTS

Instructions: Begin with one leg of the pants. With smaller dpn, CO 28 (32, 40) sts; join, being careful not to twist cast-on row. Knit 7 rnds.

Change to larger dpn and inc on the next rnd with k1f&b into every 4th st = 35 (40, 50) sts.
Knit 3 rnds. On the next rnd, inc with k1f&b into every 5th st = 42 (48, 60) sts.
Knit 14 (17, 20) rnds. At beginning of next rnd, BO 4 (6, 8) and then knit the rem sts onto two larger dpn 19 (21, 26) sts on each of the 2 dpn. Set sts aside while you work the other leg the same way.

Place the legs with the bound-off sections facing each other onto larger dpn or short circular and join them by knitting all the sts. Knit 2 more rnds = 76 (84, 104) sts total.
On every other rnd, k2tog 2 times at center front and center back 3 (3, 4) times = 64 (72, 88) sts. Knit 3 (5, 10) rnds.

Change to smaller dpn and work (k2, k2tog) around = 48 (54, 66) sts rem. Knit 3 rnds.

Make a lace rnd for the elastic casing: K 0 (2, 2), *yo, k2tog*; rep * to * around.

Knit 1 rnd, purl 1 rnd and then BO. Weave in all yarn tails on WS and seam the gap where the legs meet. Thread elastic through lace row casing.

> The light blue tunic and pants set is knit with Rowan's 4-ply Organic Cotton.

Coat

You can vary the style of the coat by choosing among collar shapes. A pointed collar is more suited for a boy bear while the rounded collar is favored by girls. You'll find the patterns on page 60.

Yarn: Choose yarn recommended for US sizes 1.5 and 2.5 / 2.5 and 3 mm. We used yarn with 145-219 yds / 133-200 m/50 g. It's a big range but, since the pattern is based on rows, not inch/cm measurements, substituting yarns is not a problem.
Needles: A short circular and set of 5 dpn US size 2.5 / 3 mm or 1.5 / 2.5mm if you knit loosely.
Notions: 2-2-3 buttons for the coat.

Before You Knit: The coat is worked back and forth, beginning at lower edge. The sleeves are worked down from the armholes and the collar is knit last.

Instructions: CO 85 (103, 121) sts and knit 1 ridge (= 2 rows)

Large Size:
Knit pattern A 0 (0, 9) rows.
On next row, K4, *k2tog, k5, ssk, k4*; rep * to * across = 103 sts rem for large. Work the row 2 of pattern B first, and then follow the instructions for the medium size below.

Medium Size (Large continues here):
Work pattern B 0 (6, 8) rows.
On next row, dec as follows: K4, *k2tog, k3, ssk, k4*; rep * to * across = 85 sts rem for all sizes.

Small Size (Large and Medium continue here):
Work pattern C 7 (7, 7) rows.
Next row: K4, *k2tog, k1, ssk, k4*; rep * to * across = 67 sts rem.

All sizes:
Work pattern D 7 (7, 7) rows. The first 3 sts of the next row are for making a buttonhole: K1, yo, ssk, knit rem sts across (= row 2 of pattern D).

Now each size is described separately.

Small
Work pattern D 5 more rows.
On next row, dec as follows: K4, *sl 1-k2tog-psso, k4*; rep * to * across = 49 sts rem.
Work row 1 of pattern E once.
Make buttonhole over the first 3 sts of row 2, k9, BO 2, k21, BO 2, and k12 = back and front.
Continue with pattern E, working back and front separately (see instructions on next page).

Medium
Work row 1 of pattern D once more.
Dec on the next row: K4, *k2tog, k5*; rep * to * across = 58 sts rem. Work pattern F 3 rows.
Make buttonhole and shape underarm on next row: Make buttonhole over the first 3 sts, k10, BO 4, k24, BO 4, K13. Now work each side separately in pattern F (see page 60).

Large

Knit 5 more rows of pattern D and, on the next row, make a buttonhole. Work row 1 of pattern D once. The next row is the RS (row 2 of pattern D); shape underarms: K15, BO 6, k25, BO6, k15.

The back and front and now worked separately in pattern D.

All Sizes

First front: First work the front where the yarn is attached (side without buttonholes). Work 6 (4, 6) rows or until you can count 3 ridges from the underarm shaping.

Neck: BO the first 3 sts and work rest of row in pattern. On the next row, work to last 2 sts and k2tog at neck edge. Dec the same way at neck edge on every RS row until 6 sts rem for shoulder. Continue in pattern for 2 more rows and then knit 1 row and BO.

Back: Work in pattern until you can count 7 (8, 10) ridges without any shaping. Knit 1 row and BO.

Other front: Begin on WS and work 3 rows in pattern.

Make a buttonhole over the first 3 sts and then complete row + 3 more pattern rows. BO 3 sts at beg on next RS row and then k2tog at beg of every other row until 6 sts rem. Work 4 (2, 2) more pattern rows, knit 1 row and then BO.

Weave in all yarn tails on WS and join shoulders.

Sleeves: Begin at center of underarm. With dpn, pick up and knit 27 (30, 39) sts. Divide the sts over 3 dpn as you knit 1 rnd over all the sts.

The two smaller sizes do not have any armhole shaping. Shape armholes for large as follows: K2tog at beg and end of the next 3 RS rows (= 33 sts rem). Work in sleeve pattern for 16 (16, 20) rows or until you can count 8 (8, 10) ridges from the row where you picked

Page 58

up sts for the sleeve.
Now (knit 1 rnd, purl 1 rnd) 6 times and then BO. Make the other sleeve the same way.

Choose a Pointed or Round Collar

Round Collar: With WS facing, pick up and knit 26 (32, 36) sts around neck; begin and end inside the 3 sts for the buttonhole/button bands at each side. Knit 3 ridges (= 6 rows).
On the next row, inc with k1f&b in every other st = 39 (48, 54) sts. Knit 3 (5, 5) rows. K2tog at beg of the next 4 rows and then BO.

Pointed Collar: With WS facing, pick up and knit 26 (32, 36) sts around neck; begin and end inside the 3 sts for the buttonhole/button bands at each side. Knit 3 ridges.
K1f&b into first st, k2; rep * to * across. Inc the same way into the first st of every row as you work 8 or 12 rows, depending on how large of a collar you want. BO.

Weave in yarn tails on WS and sew buttons onto coat. Lightly steam press coat under a pressing cloth or towel to make the pattern even and smooth.

Page 59

Pattern A

Begin here for Large.
Row 1: K3, *p1, k9, p1, k2.* Rep * to * until 14 sts rem and end p1, k9, p1, k3.
Row 2: Knit across.

Pattern B

Begin here for Medium; continue for Large.
Row 1: Knit.
Row 2: K3, *p1, k7, p1, k2.* Rep * to * until 12 sts rem and end p1, k7, p1, k3.

Pattern C

Row 1: K3, *p1, k5, p1, k2.* Rep * to * until 10 sts rem and end p1, k5, p1, k3.
Row 2: Knit.

Pattern D

Row 1: K3, *p1, k3, p1, k2.* Rep * to * until 8 sts rem and end p1, k3, p1, k3.
Row 2: Knit.

Pattern E

Row 1: K3, *p1, k1, p1, k2.* Rep * to * until 3 sts rem and end k3.
Row 2: Knit.

Pattern F

Row 1: K3, *p1, k2.* Rep * to * until 3 sts rem and end k3.
Row 2: Knit.

Sleeve pattern

Rnd 1: (P2, k1) around.
Rnd 2: Knit.

Buttonhole

K1, yo, ssk.

The smallest coat is knitted with dove-blue Rowan 4-ply Cotton (186 yds / 170 m/50 g, color 145). You'll need only .9 oz / 26 g for the small size.

The blue coat for the large bear and the pink coat for the medium teddy are both knit with Garnstudio's Silk-Tweed. The yarn has 219 yds / 200 m/50 g. The blue is color 27 and the pink color 15. The blue coat uses 1.6 oz / 46 g and the pink one 1.3 oz / 37 g.

The white coat is knit with Baby Silk from Du Store Alpakka. The yarn has 145 yds / 133 m/50 g and you'll need 2 oz / 58 g, just a little more than 1 skein.

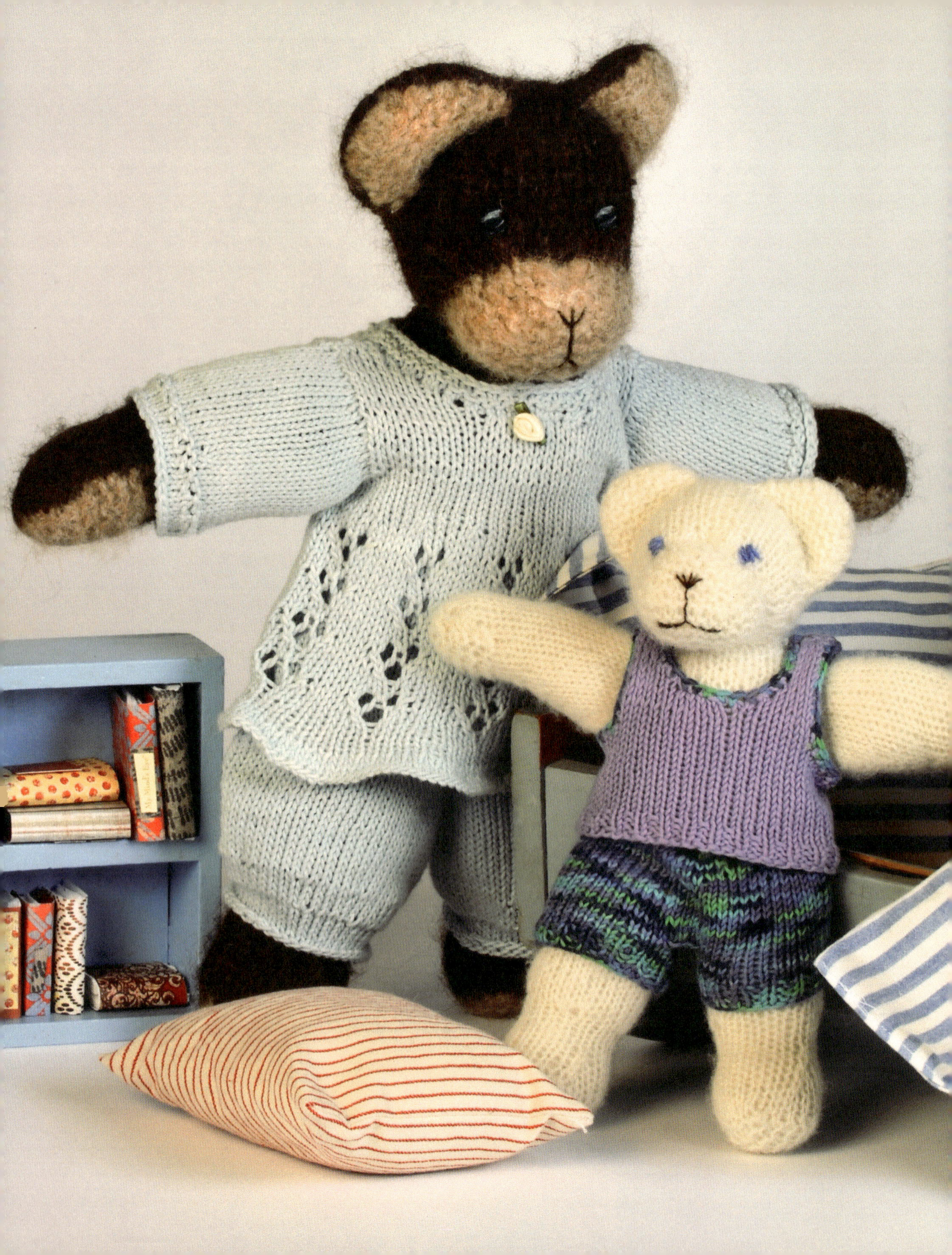

Knitting Techniques

Explanations of Terms and Techniques Used in this Book

A ridge: Garter stitch ridges are made with all knit rows when working back and forth and alternating knit and purl rounds if working in the round. A ridge looks like a knit row followed by a purl ridge as seen on the RS. 1 garter ridge = 2 knit rows or 1 knit + 1 purl round.

Stockinette: If you are working back and forth, knit on the RS and purl on the WS. If you are working around on a circular needle or dpn, all rounds are knitted.

Yarnover (yo): Make a new stitch by bringing the yarn over the needle from the back and forward and then work the next stitch as usual. Sometimes a yarnover is paired with k2tog. That means an increase with the yarnover and a decrease with k2tog so that the total stitch count is not changed.

What does * to * mean? When you see *…* in a pattern, it means that you should repeat the stitch sequence within the asterisks several times until no more sts remain on the row/round. Sometimes you might see, for example: rep * to * until 3 sts rem. That means that you work the stitch sequence within the asterisks until 3 sts are left at the end of the row or round.

Knit 2 together (k2tog): Insert the right needle knitwise into 2 sts at the same time (needle tip goes into the 2nd st from left ndl tip first and then into the 1st st) and knit them together as if they were one stitch. This makes a right-leaning decrease.

Slip-Slip-Knit (ssk): Slip the first st from the left to the right needle as if to knit and then slip the 2nd st knitwise onto right needle. Insert left needle into loops and knit together through back loops. This makes a left-leaning decrease. K2tog and ssk are often used in combination to make mirror-image shaping lines.

Knitted Cast-on: Knit 1 st into a cast-on loop or the first st of a row and place the new st back on the left needle without slipping the stitch worked into off left needle. Knit into the new stitch, place it on left needle without slipping the old stitch off. Continue the same way until you have the number of stitches specified. This cast-on method is recommended whenever you need an elastic cast-on edge or for adding stitches at the side of the knitting.

Increase with Knit 1 front and back (k1f&b): Knit 1 st as usual but do not slip the old stitch off left needle. Make another stitch by working into back loop.

Increase with Make 1 (m1): Insert the left needle under the strand between 2 stitches and lift the yarn up to the needle as a stitch. Knit this new stitch into the back loop before proceeding to rem sts.

Twisted Knit: A knit stitch with its loop twisted around the needle. The part of the knit stitch that faces you

Page 63

is the front leg of the stitch and we usually insert the needle under it from left to right when we knit a stitch. The part of the stitch that sits behind the needle is the back leg of the stitch. If you knit into the back leg (inserting needle from right to left) instead of the front one, you have made a twisted knit.

Picking Up and Knitting Stitches along a Knitted Edge: Insert the needle into a stitch as if to knit and bring yarn around needle and through loop to form a new stitch.

Counting Stitches and Rows: Imagine the knit stitch as a V and the purl stitch as a dash - . Count the V's and dashes across when you count stitches and up when you count rows. To make it easier for a precise count, I like to use the tip of the needle to count up/across.

Yardage: This is how many yards / meters are in, for example, 2.2 pounds / 1 kilo of yarn. Yarn is usually sold in balls or skeins weighing 1 ¾ oz / 50 g so the yarns listed in this book are given in terms of yards and meters in 50 g.

Acknowledgements

Thank you to Marit Ulset and Solfrid Sørensen who each knitted their own bear with clothes.

Thanks to Tove Balas for doing the book layout and to photographer Sidsel Jørgensen for the pictures. Thanks also to Carol Rhoades for translating this book into English. Without their input, this book would not have been as good.

Thanks to Mary-Ann, Sonja, Gunn, Torgeir and Øystein for their constructive insights and inspiration during the progress of the book.

Thanks to the people who work in the yarn shops "Karmin Yarn and Gifts AS" and "Lars Langfeldt AS" in Kristiansand, Norway, and "Blå Tråd" [Blue Yarn] in Arendal for inspiring knitting conversations and useful information about yarn choices for the bears and their clothes.

Thanks also to everyone else in knitting shops all around Norway who so willingly impart their knowledge and enthusiasm. I haven't met all of them but highly value their deep knowledge that they share with their customers.

Thanks to the shop "Den Blaa Dør" [The Blue Door] in Kristiansand for the loan of the dresser and bench to photograph with the bears and for the many lovely conversations about knitting and a little of everything throughout the years!

Resources

The yarn for knitting the bears and clothes in this book are available from these companies. Check their websites for retailers in your area.

Rowan Yarn
www.knitrowan.com

SandnesGarn AS
www.sandnesgarn.no; distributed in the U.S. by
www.swedishyarn.com

Du Store Alpakka
www.dustorealpakka.com; a similar range of yarns is available in the U.S. from
www.blueskyalpacas.com

Rauma Ullvarefabrikk AS
www.raumaull.no ; distributed in the U.S. by
www.nordicfiberarts.com

DROPS Design Garnstudio
www.garnstudio.com

Rauma Ullvarefabrikk AS and Hillesvåg Ullvarefabrikk AS
(Washed and carded wool)
www.hifa.no

www.tonetakle.com
www.tonetakle.no

Your own Notes

Printed in Great Britain
by Amazon.co.uk, Ltd.,
Marston Gate.